Boats

written by Wendy Graham

Engage Literacy is published in 2013 by Raintree.
Raintree is an imprint of Capstone Global Library Limited, a company incorporated in Engand and Wales having its registered office at 7 Pilgrim Street, London, EC4V 6LB – Registered company number: 6695582
www.raintreepublishers.co.uk

Originally published in Australia by Hinkler Education, a division of Hinkler Books Pty Ltd.
Text and illustration copyright © Hinkler Books Pty Ltd 2012

Written by Wendy Graham
Lead authors Jay Dale and Anne Giulieri
Illustrations pp 6, 11, 23–24 by Gaston Vanzet
Edited by Gwenda Smyth
UK edition edited by Dan Nunn, Catherine Veitch and Sian Smith
Designed by Susannah Low, Butterflyrocket Design

All rights reserved. No part of this publication may be reproduced, stored in a retrieval system, or transmitted in any way or by any means, electronic, mechanical, photocopying, recording or otherwise, without the prior written permission of Capstone Global Library Limited.

Boats
ISBN: 978 1 406 26543 9
10 9 8 7 6 5 4 3 2 1

Printed and bound in China by Leo Paper Products Ltd

Acknowledgements
Cover images (left to right): iStockphoto.com/ © James Steidl; © Veronica Wools | Dreamstime.com; © Yuriykulik | Dreamstime.com; Glow Images/Prisma/Otto Werner.; p4 top (and title page): © Veronica Wools | Dreamstime.com; p4 second from top: © Gordan Poropat | Dreamstime.com; p4 middle: © Ivan Cholakov | Dreamstime.com; p4 bottom left: © Nadiya Kravchenko | Dreamstime.com; p4 bottom right (and Contents page top): © Alptraum | Dreamstime.com; p5 top: © Baloncici | Dreamstime.com; p5 bottom: © Felics | Dreamstime.com; p6 top right: © Dalibor Sevaljevic | Dreamstime.com; p7 top left: iStockphoto.com/ © Damir Spanic; p7 top right: iStockphoto.com/ © Brian Palmer; p7 bottom: Glow Images/ © Ariel Skelley/CORBIS; p8: Getty Images/Stockbyte; p9 top left: Glow Images/Prisma/Otto Werner; p9 top right: © Age Fotostock / SuperStock; p9 bottom: © Lianem | Dreamstime.com; p10: © Glenda Powers | Dreamstime.com; p12 top (and Contents page bottom): © Yuriykulik | Dreamstime.com; p12 middle: © Tom Dowd | Dreamstime.com; p12 bottom: Onne van der Wal / Bluegreenpictures.com; p13 top: © Gina Smith | Dreamstime.com; p13 middle: iStockphoto.com/ © Brian Palmer; p13 bottom: © Will Iredale | Dreamstime.com; p14: © Newspix / News Ltd / James Kerr; p15 top: Imagebroker.net/SuperStock; p15 middle: © Julie Feinstein | Dreamstime.com; p15 bottom: iStockphoto.com/ © egdigital; p16 top: © Jennifer Pitiquen | Dreamstime.com; p16 middle: © Sanches1980 | Dreamstime.com; p16 bottom: © Nigel Spiers | Dreamstime.com; p17 top: iStockphoto.com/ © David Joyner; p17 middle: © Sebastian Czapnik | Dreamstime.com; p17 bottom: Courtesy Irish Ferries; p18 top: © Michele Cornelius | Dreamstime.com; p18 bottom: iStockphoto.com/ © Peter Leyden; p19 top left: © Nattesha | Dreamstime.com; p19 top right: Tetra Images/SuperStock; p19 bottom: Transtock/SuperStock; p20: iStockphoto.com/ © choicegraphx; p21 left (and back cover): iStockphoto.com/ © Dan Barnes; p21 right: iStockphoto.com/ © Oytun Karadayi; p22 left: iStockphoto.com/ © James Steidl; p22 right: © Alex Zarubin | Dreamstime.com; p23 top left: © Farek | Dreamstime.com; p23 top right: © Alvera | Dreamstime.com; p23 bottom left: © Marzanna Syncerz | Dreamstime.com; p23 bottom right: © Kostyantyn Ratnikov | Dreamstime.com

Contents

Introduction	4
Fishing Boats	6
Trawlers	8
Sailing Boats	10
Yachts	12
Police Boats	14
Water Taxis	16
Ferries	17
Tugboats	18
Ocean Barges	19
Cargo Ships	20
Ocean Liners	22
Picture Glossary	24

Introduction

There are many different kinds of boats. Some boats, such as sailing boats, need wind in their sails to move. Large ships, however, use *powerful engines* to move through the sea.

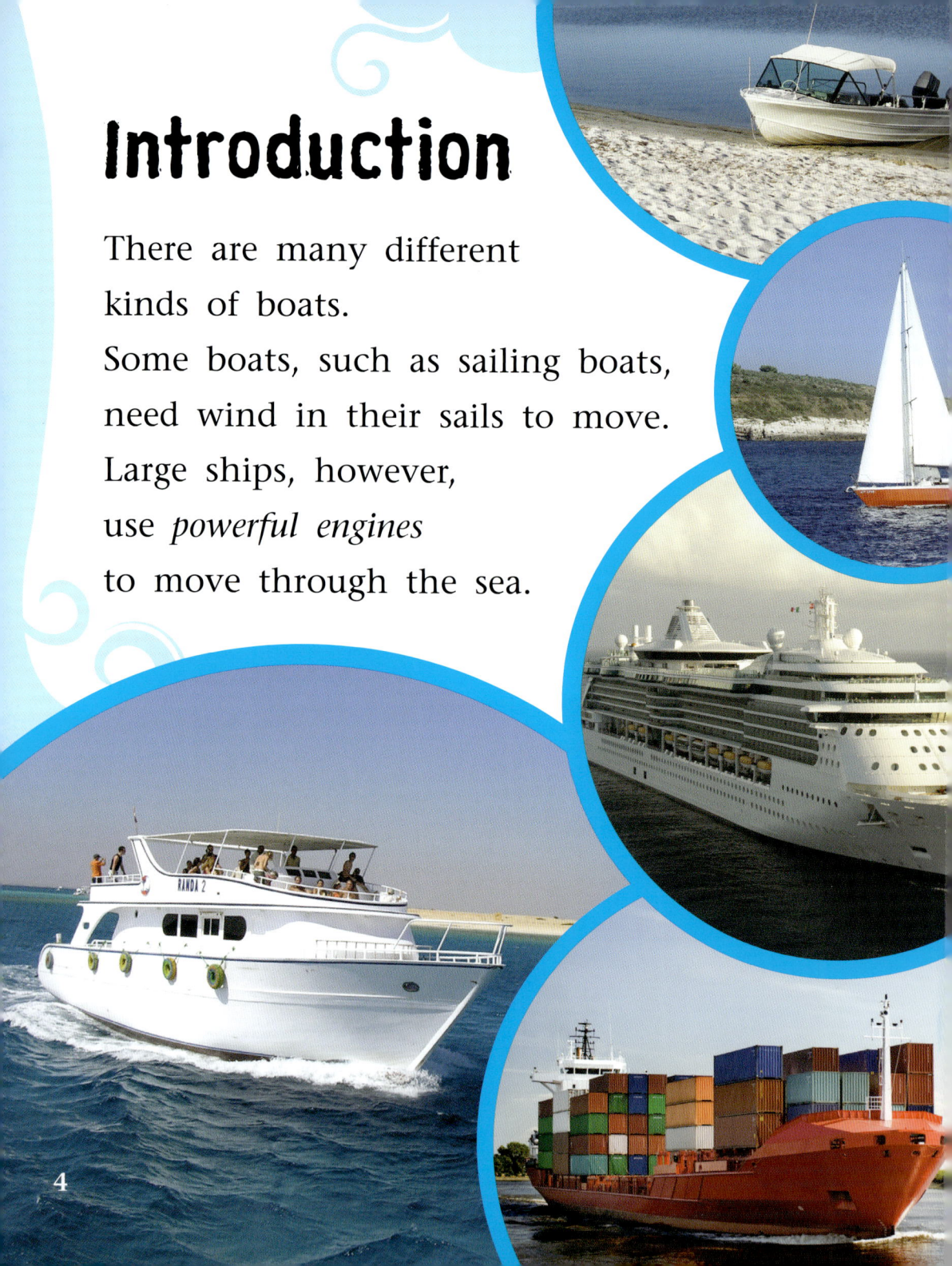

Some boats are used for fun, for travel or for fishing. Others are used for work or to move *goods* from place to place.

In this book, you will read about many different kinds of boats.

There are about 38,000 ships or boats on the world's oceans at any one time.

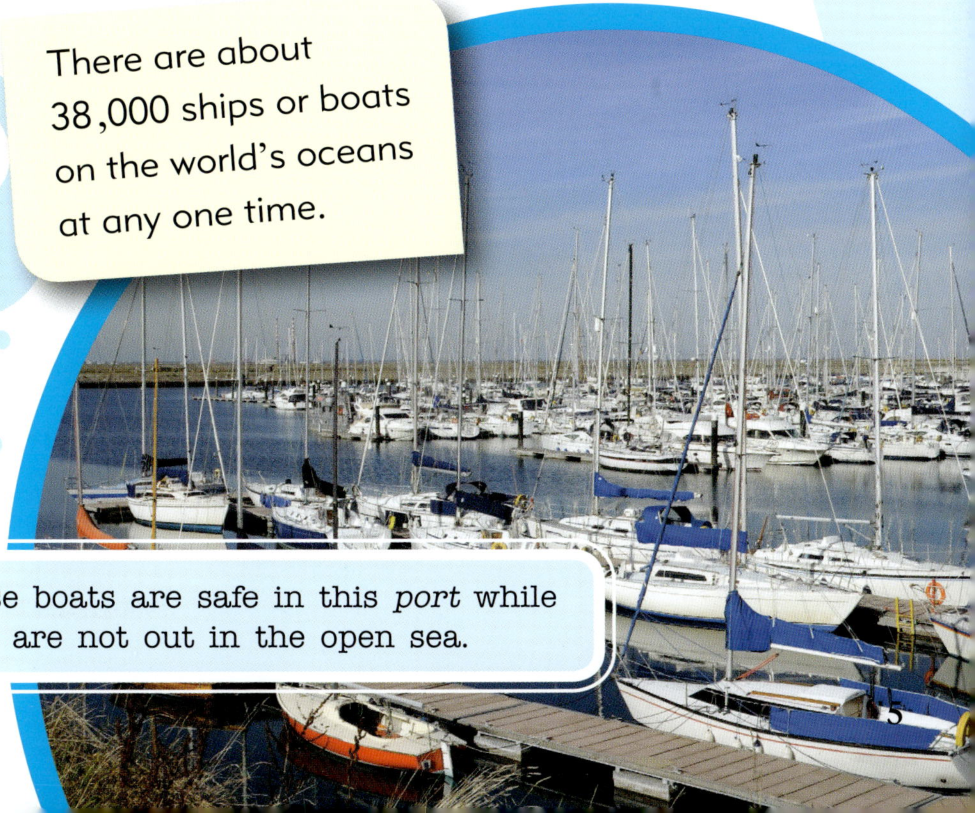

These boats are safe in this *port* while they are not out in the open sea.

Fishing Boats

There are many different kinds of fishing boats. Some fishing boats are small and have *benches* for people to sit on. These boats use a small motor to move through the sea.

Some fishing boats are small enough to go on a car's roof.

Some small fishing boats are made of metal while others are made of wood.

Some larger fishing boats stay out at sea for days or weeks. These boats have bunks for people to sleep in and a tiny kitchen called a galley.

It is important that people wear life jackets on a small boat and do not move suddenly or jump about.

Trawlers

Some people's job is to catch fish. They use a boat called a *trawler*. Trawlers pull special nets through the sea to catch fish. Some trawlers are small boats while others are large. They have an engine room, bunks and a galley.

Large fishing trawlers catch lots of fish in their nets.

Some trawlers have special *machines* for lifting heavy nets full of fish up onto the *deck*.

Fish that are caught are kept cold in ice or seawater.

Sailing Boats

Some people enjoy sailing for fun. A sailing boat skims across the top of the water. When the wind hits its sails, the boat is pushed along.

People sail for sport, too. You can race sailing boats all year round. People can go to sailing school to learn how to sail.

Yachts

Large sailing boats
are called yachts.
They are light and fast-moving.
The wind in their sails
moves them across the sea.
Some people race their yachts.

Sometimes people use
their yacht as their home
when they travel
from place to place.

A very large yacht is called
a mega sailing yacht.
It has many cabins and
can carry up to 50 people.

Larger yachts have a cabin for sleeping, a galley and a bathroom.

Most yachts have motors. These are used when there is very little wind or they come into a *jetty*.

Police Boats

Some police officers work on police boats. Police boats have very powerful engines, so they can move swiftly across the water. Police boats have *sirens* and flashing lights just like police cars.

Some police boats have police divers who dive underwater.

Police officers on police boats work very hard to keep our waters safe.

Most large cities with ports have police boats.

Most police boats are very fast!

Water Taxis

Water taxis are boats that take people a short distance across the water. They might carry a few people or they might carry as many as 40 people. The seating area is sometimes covered so people do not get wet in rainy weather. There are also outside areas where people can enjoy the sunshine.

Water taxis can be used to take people to work, to an island or to a boat.

Some water taxis can land right on the beach.

Ferries

Ferries are much larger than water taxis. They carry a large number of people from one place to another. Ferries usually arrive and leave at the same time every day. Some ferries have upstairs and downstairs areas so they can carry more people. Some even have places to eat and cabins where people can sleep.

Many ferries carry cars, trucks and buses.

The world's largest ferry is called a superferry.
It can carry about 1340 cars, 240 trucks and 2000 people.

Tugboats

Even though tugboats are small, they are very powerful. They push or tow boats that cannot move under their own power. Sometimes, when a boat is stuck in *shallow* water, a tugboat will pull it out. Most tugboats have a *crew* of four people.

Small tugboats can tow huge ships in or out of a busy port.

Tugs are so strongly built that they can be used as ice-breakers. Ice-breakers are boats that push through water that is full of ice.

Ocean Barges

Most ocean barges have a large, flat deck. They carry all kinds of things such as cars, *machinery*, rubbish and other heavy items.

Other ocean barges do special jobs such as *dredging* or laying pipes beneath the sea.

Cargo Ships

Cargo ships move goods such as furniture, cars and food to different parts of the world.

Cargo ships are also called container ships.

Containers are giant metal boxes that hold goods for transport. The containers can hold many different kinds of goods such as clothes or TV sets. These are loaded onto the cargo ship at a place called a port.

One cargo ship can carry many containers.

Ocean Liners

Many people go on ocean liners for holidays. Ocean liners are sometimes called cruise ships. They travel all around the world. These large ships have *restaurants*, swimming pools and even *cinemas*. There are often thousands of people on board.

Ocean liners have many decks with cabins for sleeping.

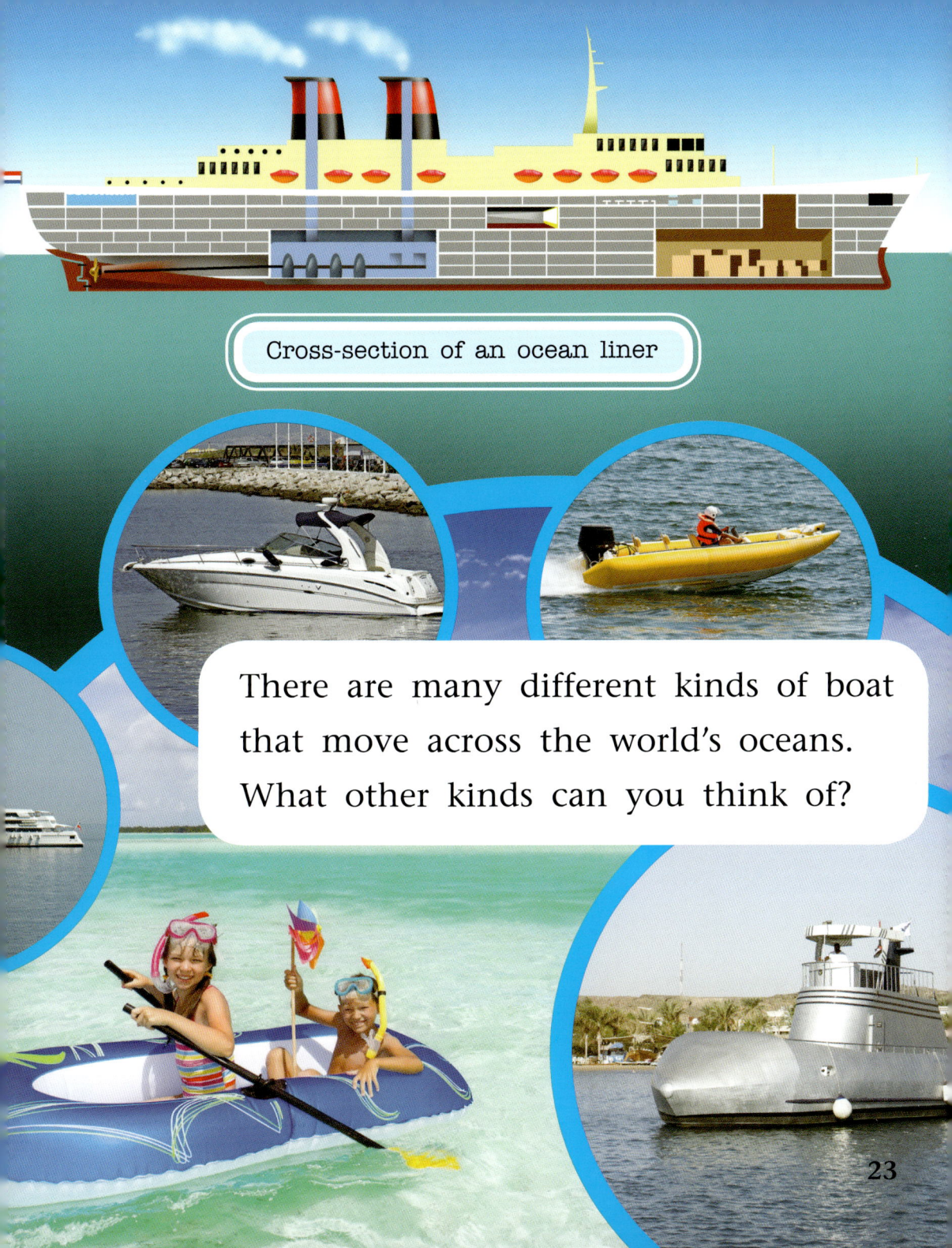

Cross-section of an ocean liner

There are many different kinds of boat that move across the world's oceans. What other kinds can you think of?

23

Picture Glossary

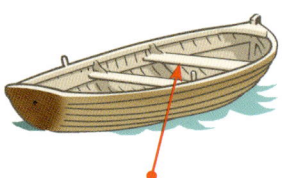 benches

 powerful engines

 restaurants

 cinemas

 goods

 shallow

 crew

 jetty

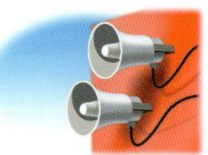 sirens

 deck

 machines/machinery

 trawler

 dredging

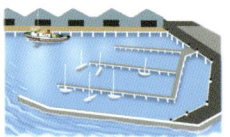 port